I0167522

A Wide World of Vertebrates

This course was written by
Naturally Curious Expert
Tucker Hirsch

*Tucker is a marine scientist who is curious about
the lives and future of our ocean friends.*

Printed by CreateSpace

ISBN 978-1-942403-05-0

www.benaturallycurious.com

Many activities in this book make use of printed materials. If you prefer not to cut them directly from this book, please visit the URL listed below and enter the code for a supplemental PDF containing all printable materials.

URL: www.benaturallycurious.com/vertebrates-printables/

password: **backbone**

Table of Contents

Required materials: Scissors, string, hanger, hole punch, colored pencils, crayons, or markers, pennies, M&Ms, Cheerios, dry beans, buttons (or similar), brass fastener, glue, paper plate or cardboard, paper clip, 5 colors of chalk, timer (up to 2 minutes)

Devi the Dolphin

"Whee!" cried Devi as she splashed back into the water. "I love practicing backflips!" Devi is a dolphin. She lives in the ocean. Devi takes gymnastics.

"That flip was perfect, Devi. Great work. I can tell you've been practicing," Devi's gymnastics teacher told her. "I think we're all done for today. Your dad will be here soon to pick you up."

"Thank you!" responded Devi. "Can I ask you a question?"

"**O**f course, Devi."

"I noticed that some of my friends can't do backflips. My friends the sea stars and jellies can barely even swim. They never catch me when we play tag. Why can't they move like I can?" asked Devi.

Devi's teacher answered, "That's a great question, Devi. You can swim, jump, flip, and move so well because you are a **VERTEBRATE**. And like all vertebrates, you have a backbone. Your friends the sea stars and jellies don't have backbones. They are **INVERTEBRATES**. Your bones support your body and muscles, which helps you grow and be strong. That's why you can move so quickly and easily."

"So, animals are either vertebrates or invertebrates?" Devi wondered out loud.

"Yes. That's right. Vertebrates have backbones. Invertebrates do not. As a matter of fact, invertebrates don't have any bones at all!" Devi's teacher explained.

Vertebrates are animals with backbones.

Animals are either *vertebrates* or *invertebrates*.

Take a look at some of Devi's friends. Can you sort them into two categories: vertebrates and invertebrates? Most animals on Earth are actually invertebrates. Some of them have soft, squishy bodies. Other invertebrates have hard, stiff bodies, like most of Devi's sea star friends. But sea stars and corals can't move very well. They don't have a backbone to support very much movement. Vertebrates' bodies have much more structure, and because of their backbones, they can usually move around much better. Circle the animals you think are vertebrates. Cross out the animals you think are invertebrates. (Answers are on page 25.)

> **M**ost animals on Earth are *invertebrates*.

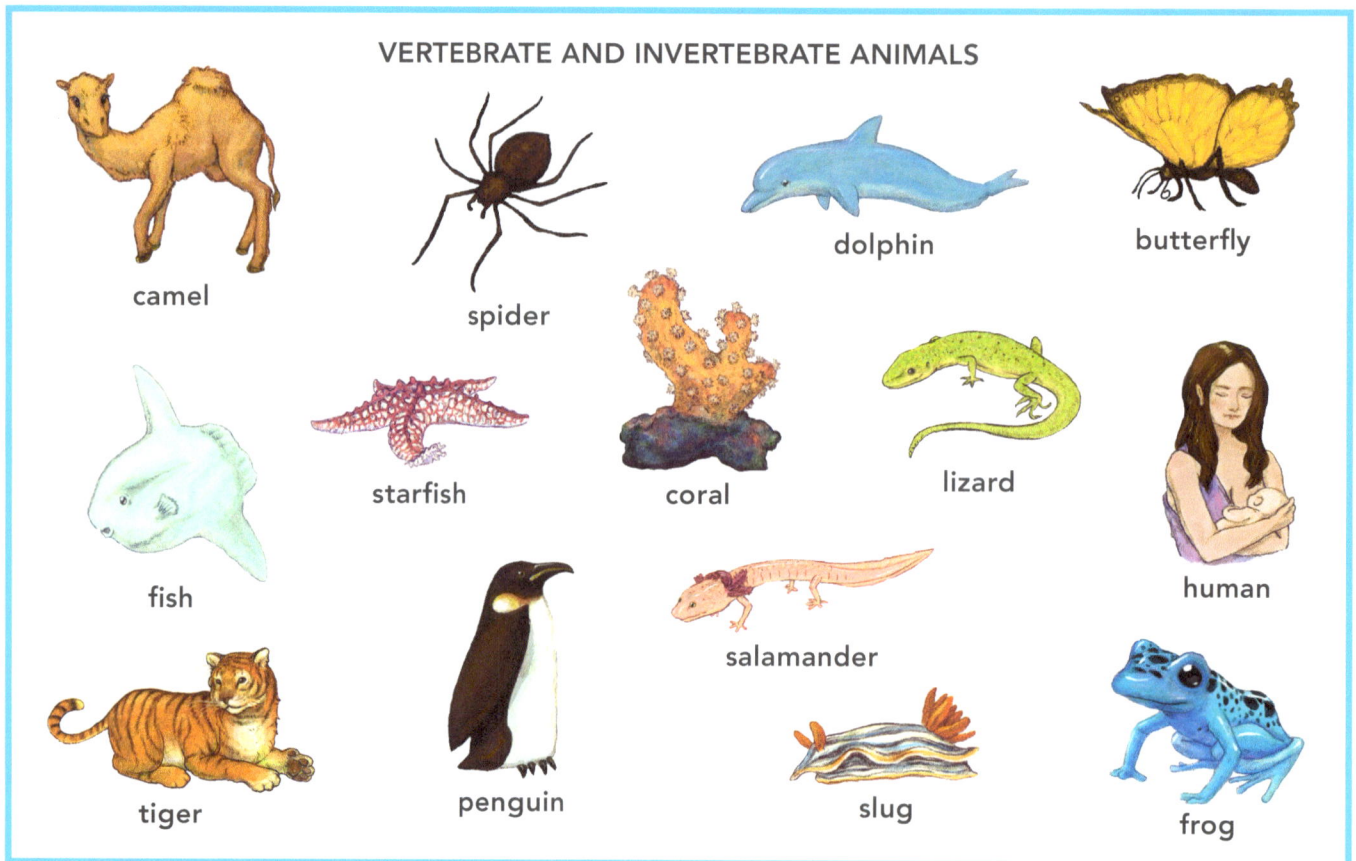

VERTEBRATE AND INVERTEBRATE ANIMALS

camel

spider

dolphin

butterfly

fish

starfish

coral

lizard

human

tiger

penguin

salamander

slug

frog

How did you do? Some animals are tricky. Spiders and butterflies are invertebrates, even though they have hard bodies and can move quickly. Salamanders and frogs have soft bodies but still have a backbone inside to help them move. Let's see how Devi's doing with the new vocabulary she learned.

> **V**ertebrates can usually move around much better than *invertebrates*.

"I'm a little confused," confessed Devi. "If so many of my friends are *vertebrates*, how come we are so different from each other? My friend the seagull has wings and can fly. I live in the ocean, but I have to come to the surface to breathe air. My friend Freddie the Flounder, a fish, swims like me but has scales and breathes underwater. Why are we all so different if we're all vertebrates?"

To answer this question, Devi's teacher drew a chart. Look at your chart on page 12 and fill it out along with Devi. Scientists place all vertebrates into five categories:

Amphibians	Birds	Fish	Mammals	Reptiles

The one thing all groups have in common is their backbone. Within each group, the animals share certain CHARACTERISTICS. Characteristics are things we can notice about an animal's body or its behavior. Devi's teacher asked her what she knew about the different groups.

"I know what BIRDS are," Devi said. "They all have feathers, and most of them fly. I know that FISH live and breathe underwater, and they have scales. But I don't know what the other groups are."

"That's a good start," Devi's teacher responded. "Let's fill in the chart with what you do know. And since you know that fish breathe in the water, we can also include that birds breathe air out of water. Fish use gills to get oxygen from the water. Birds get oxygen from the air with their lungs."

Vertebrates are divided into five groups: fish, birds, mammals, reptiles, and amphibians.

Animals in each group share *characteristics*.

Amphibians	Birds	Fish	Mammals	Reptiles
	feathers lungs	scales gills		

BIRDS AND FISH

"You, Devi, are a MAMMAL," her teacher explained.

"I thought I was a vertebrate! And a dolphin! How can I be a mammal?" Devi was getting confused.

"You are all three," the teacher said. "The group you fit into is mammals, just like all the other dolphins and whales in the ocean. Many land animals are also mammals."

"Because we breathe air?" asked Devi.

Her teacher said, "Because you breathe air with your lungs, and a few other things. All mammals have lungs. They are also WARM-BLOODED. This means that when the air or water around you is very cold, your body stays warm on the inside. And when it gets very hot, your body doesn't overheat. You can control your own body temperature and keep it warm enough but not too warm. Your temperature doesn't change that much." Devi added this new information to the chart.

Amphibians	Birds	Fish	Mammals	Reptiles
	feathers lungs	scales gills	**lungs warm-blooded**	

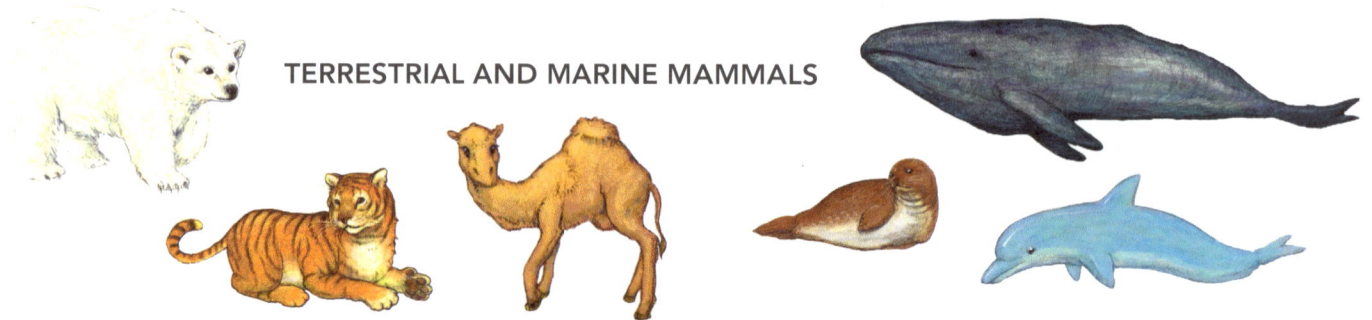

TERRESTRIAL AND MARINE MAMMALS

"Okay, but what about eggs? My friend the seagull said she hatched from an egg! I did NOT hatch from an egg. People don't hatch from eggs, either. They come out of hospitals!" Devi exclaimed.

What are you CURIOUS about?

Devi's teacher laughed. "Humans, whales, dolphins, and almost all mammals are born live, from their mothers. They don't hatch from eggs. But you're right—birds lay eggs. We can add that to our chart, too. Mammals give birth to live young, and birds lay eggs. Most fish lay eggs, but some fish give birth to live young."

Amphibians	Birds	Fish	Mammals	Reptiles
	feathers lungs **lay eggs**	scales gills **lay eggs (usually)**	lungs warm-blooded **give birth to live young**	

Birds and fish lay eggs.

Mammals have live young.

"Wow!" Devi said. "Our chart is growing. What else is special about mammals?"

"A few more things," her teacher went on. "Mammal babies drink milk from their mothers. And they all have hair. Somewhere on their bodies, at some point in their lives, all mammals have hair. When you were born, you had a few hairs on your chin, but they fell out soon after."

"More for our chart!" Devi said, excited.

Amphibians	Birds	Fish	Mammals	Reptiles
	feathers lungs lay eggs	scales gills lay eggs (usually)	**hair/fur** lungs warm-blooded give birth to live young **drink mother's milk**	

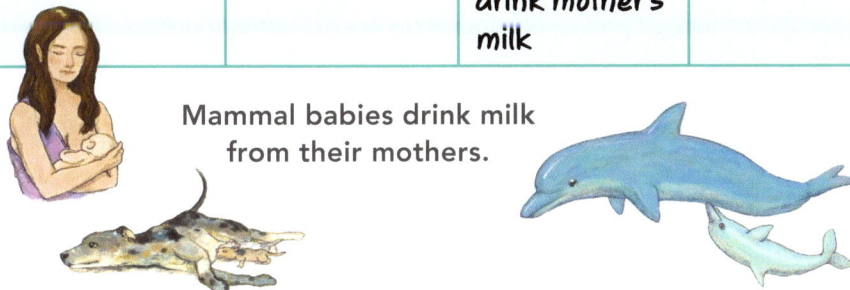

**Mammal babies drink milk
from their mothers.**

"But we still have lots of holes in our chart. What do baby birds drink? And are fish warm-blooded like me?" Devi asked.

Her teacher laughed. "Birds are warm-blooded like you. Fish, on the other hand, are COLD-BLOODED. They don't actually have cold blood, but they can't control their body temperatures. If they are in a place that is too cold or hot, their bodies get too cold or hot. They can even die if their surroundings get very cold or hot. And no, they do not have hair. We already talked about birds' feathers and fishes' scales. Their mothers don't have MAMMARY GLANDS, the body parts that make the milk. So their babies can't drink milk. Go ahead and add those facts to your chart."

Amphibians	Birds	Fish	Mammals	Reptiles
	feathers	scales	hair/fur	
	lungs	gills	lungs	
	warm-blooded	**cold-blooded**	warm-blooded	
	lay eggs	lay eggs (usually)	give birth to live young	
	X	X	drink mother's milk	

YOUNG BIRDS AND FISH

"So, now you know all there is to know about birds, fish, and mammals. What do you know about REPTILES and AMPHIBIANS?" Devi's teacher asked.

"Do you mean snakes and frogs?" Devi wondered.

"Sure. Snakes are a type of reptile, and frogs are a type of amphibian," her teacher added.

"Well, I know they don't have hair. And I know that most of them lay eggs. But I think that's all," Devi confessed.

"Good! You're correct. Also, their mothers don't have mammary glands, and their body coverings are different from the other vertebrates. Amphibians have smooth or slimy skin that helps them in both the land and water, while reptiles have dry, scaly skin. Add those things to your chart," her teacher instructed her.

"So...," Devi continued, "I'm going to guess that they are cold-blooded. I've seen snakes sitting in the sun to keep warm. And the frogs in the pond near the beach slow down when it gets cold."

"You're right again!" Devi's teacher said, "Reptiles and amphibians are both cold-blooded. Reptiles have lungs. You said you saw snakes sitting on rocks, so of course they can breathe out of water. Actually, they can *only* breathe out of water."

Devi asked, "But what about frogs—I mean, amphibians? Frogs sit on lily pads, but they also swim underwater. So are they air breathers, or do they breathe underwater?"

"Well, the word *amphibian* answers your question. Amphi-bian. *Amphi-* is a word that means "both," and *-bian* comes from a word that means "life." So, amphibians live both lives. As babies, amphibians breathe with their gills. As they get older, their gills disappear and their lungs develop. As adults, they breathe with lungs, and like you, they hold their breath when they swim underwater."

"Wow. Amphibians are cool. I want to add it to the chart!"

Amphibians	Birds	Fish	Mammals	Reptiles
smooth or slimy skin	feathers	scales	hair/fur	dry, scaly skin
lungs and gills	lungs	gills	lungs	lungs
cold-blooded	warm-blooded	cold-blooded	warm-blooded	cold-blooded
lay eggs (usually)	lay eggs	lay eggs (usually)	give birth to live young	lay eggs (usually)
X	X	X	drink mother's milk	X

REPTILES AND AMPHIBIANS

"Wow, Devi. You've learned a lot more than gymnastics today. Your dad's here to pick you up. Go home tonight and look over your chart. If you have any questions about the different groups of vertebrates, we can talk about it in your next class."

"Thank you!" Devi gave her teacher a high-five. "Now I will see all my friends for who they really are." Devi thanked her teacher and went home for the day. Take a look at your chart and see how it compares to Devi's chart.

MY CHART OF VERTEBRATES

Fill out the chart with Devi as you read her story.

Category	Amphibians	Birds	Fish	Mammals	Reptiles
Body covering					
How they breathe					
Warm- or cold-blooded					
Eggs or live young					
Mammary glands?					

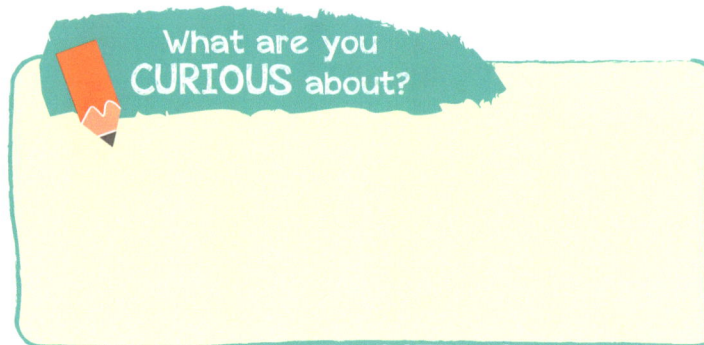

What are you CURIOUS about?

Mobile Vertebrates

ACTIVITY 1

INSTRUCTIONS

In this craft activity, you are going to make a mobile. Mobiles are hanging pieces of art. Many people put mobiles over a baby's crib. Mobiles have pretty colors, shapes, and pictures. The word *mobile* also means that something can move. A mobile home is a home that can move around, like an RV or a trailer. A mobile person is someone who moves around a lot. Vertebrates are mobile, too, because of their backbones. So, you are going to make mobile artwork of mobile animals!

1. Choose which type of vertebrate you want to use for your mobile:

   Reptiles   Birds   Mammals   Fish   Amphibians

2. Find the Vertebrate Body sheet that matches your choice (pages 29–37). Cut out each of the body parts of your chosen type of vertebrate.

3. Choose a favorite example of your type of vertebrate and draw it in the empty shape. Not sure what to choose? Check out some examples in BONES Bingo (pages 16–17) and learn more about them online.

4. Cut out the name of the group, too.

5. Next, use a hole punch (or ask an adult to help you poke a hole) to create a hole in the top of each shape.

6. Tie the pieces to the hanger with different lengths of string.

7. Hang your mobile somewhere and display it proudly!

MATERIALS

- Scissors
- String
- Hanger
- Hole punch
- Colored pencils, crayons, or markers

ACTIVITY
1

Activity Journal

Which mobile or mobiles did you create?

_____

_____

What animal or animals did you choose as your favorite(s)? Why?

_____

_____

_____

A Venn diagram is a way to compare things that are similar in some ways. In the circles below, fill in some body parts of reptiles and amphibians. For characteristics that they both have, fill in the two-colored oval in the middle, under "Both." For characteristics that only one group has, fill them in under "Reptiles" or "Amphibians."

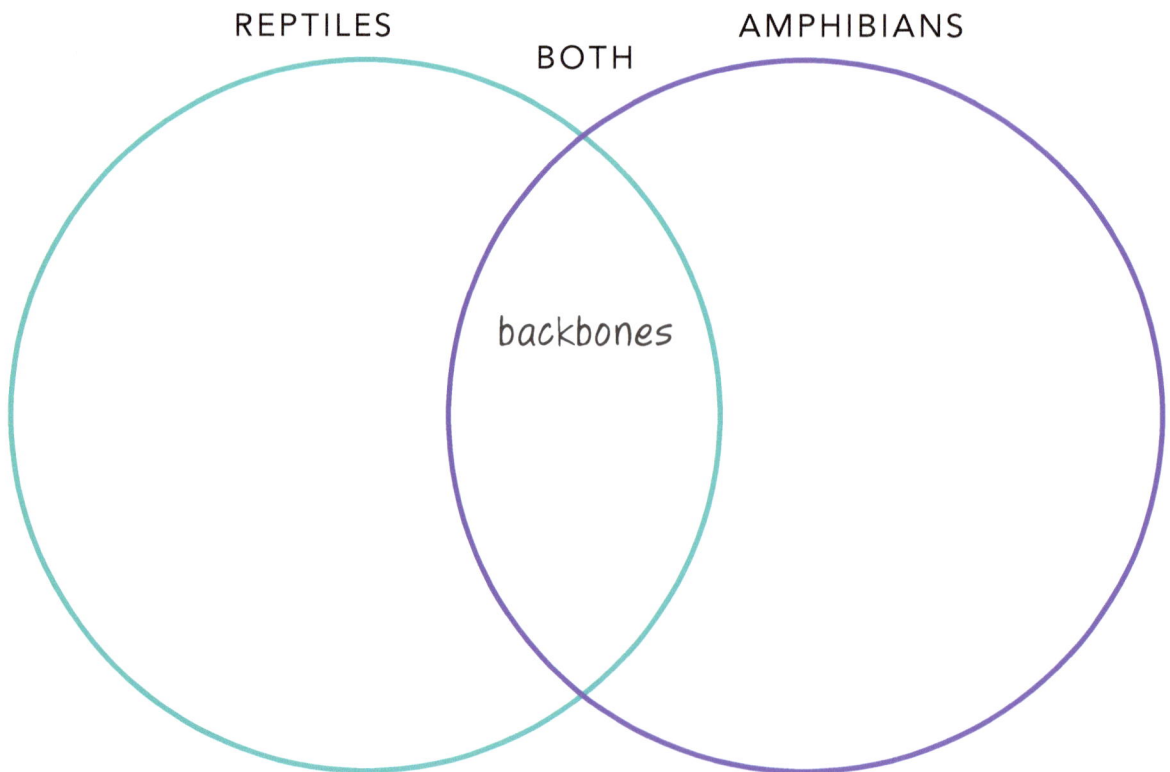

REPTILES   BOTH   AMPHIBIANS

backbones

ACTIVITY 2

BONES Bingo

INSTRUCTIONS

Now that you know about different vertebrates, test your knowledge about their body parts.

Preparation

1. Each player chooses a Vertebrate Bingo Card (pages 41 and 43).

2. Choose one person to be the caller.

3. Collect pennies or other loose change from friends and family to use as markers (remember to give it back!). You can instead use M&Ms, Cheerios, dry beans, buttons, or other small, dry items as markers.

4. Cut out the round spinner on page 39. Glue it onto a paper plate or a piece of cardboard.

5. Place a paper clip around the brass fastener. Then punch the fastener through the middle of the spinner. Don't tighten the fastener too much or the paper clip won't spin!

Parents' Tip: Don't have brass fasteners? Use some dried beans, M&M's, or something similar to gently toss onto the spinner. Each player tosses a bean during his or her turn. The caller calls out where it lands.

Playing the Game

6. Place a marker on the free space in the middle of the card.

7. The caller spins the spinner and calls out the body part or characteristic of a vertebrate.

8. Each player should first figure out which type or types of vertebrate has that body part or characteristic (using Players' Guide 1). Next, they should figure out which animals of that type they have on their card (using Players' Guide 2).

9. If you find an animal on your card with the body part, place a marker on it. Only place one marker for each body part the caller calls out.

10. The first player to get five in a row (horizontal, diagonal, or vertical) calls out BONES!

MATERIALS

- Pennies, M&Ms, Cheerios, dry beans, buttons, or similar
- Scissors
- Brass fastener
- Glue
- Paper plate or cardboard
- Paper clip

BONES Bingo

ACTIVITY
2

PLAYERS' GUIDE 1

Players can use this table to figure out which vertebrate groups have the body part or characteristic that was just called.

Category	Amphibians	Birds	Fish	Mammals	Reptiles
Body covering	X	feathers	scales	hair	X
How they breathe	gills	lungs	gills	lungs	lungs
	lungs				
Warm- or cold-blooded	cold-blooded	warm-blooded	cold-blooded	warm-blooded	cold-blooded
Eggs or live young	eggs (usually)	eggs	eggs	live young	eggs (usually)
Mammary glands?	no	no	no	yes	no
Backbone?	yes	yes	yes	yes	yes
Muscles?	yes	yes	yes	yes	yes

BONES Bingo

ACTIVITY 2

PLAYERS' GUIDE 2

Players can use this sheet to look for animals in each vertebrate group. Which animals are on your card?

Amphibians	Birds	Fish	Mammals	Reptiles
Bullfrog	Blue Jay	Angelfish	Blue Whale	American Crocodile
Frog	Eagle	Clownfish	Dog	Anaconda
Newt	Emu	Eel	Dolphin	Cane Toad
Poison Dart Frog	Flamingo	Freddie the Flounder	Human	Komodo Dragon
Salamander	Owl	Goldfish	Kangaroo	Gecko
Spotted Salamander	Pelican	Hatchetfish	Monkey	King Snake
Toad	Penguin	Mola mola	Platypus	Lizard
Warty Newt	Sparrow	Mudskipper	Pony	Sea Turtle
	Warbler	Puffer Fish	Rabbit	Snake
	Woodpecker	Shark	Tiger	Thorny Devil

ACTIVITY 2

Activity Journal

What types of vertebrates lay eggs?

_____

_____

Some vertebrates use gills to breathe. What types of vertebrates live underwater and use gills to breathe?

_____

_____

What types of vertebrates have either scales or dry, scaly skin covering their bodies?

_____

_____

Vertebrate Twister

ACTIVITY 3

INSTRUCTIONS

Use your backbone and start twisting!

Preparation

MATERIALS
- Scissors
- 5 colors of chalk
- Bingo spinner

1. Cut out and prepare (or reuse) the spinner from the Vertebrate Bingo game. (Or, if you threw a bean, have the bean and spinner handy.)

2. Cut out the circle on page 45.

3. Using the diagram below, trace the circle on the ground outside using chalk. (Check with an adult to make sure you choose an okay place to use chalk!) Make 5 circles across and 5 down. Each column should be a different color.

4. Label the circles as in the diagram below, or, make yourself a key to remember which group is represented by each color.

Reptiles	Birds	Mammals	Amphibians	Fish
Reptiles	Birds	Mammals	Amphibians	Fish
Reptiles	Birds	Mammals	Amphibians	Fish
Reptiles	Birds	Mammals	Amphibians	Fish
Reptiles	Birds	Mammals	Amphibians	Fish

ACTIVITY 3

Vertebrate Twister

INSTRUCTIONS (continued)

Parents' Tips

- You may need to test a few times to decide how far apart the circles should be. Little kids may need the circles closer together, but bigger kids can play with the circles farther apart.

- If it's too cold or you don't have a good outdoor space, consider tracing the circles on an old sheet, or paint them on a tarp or drop cloth. You could even commandeer an old Twister mat!

Playing the Game

5. Choose one person to be the caller.

6. The caller spins the spinner and calls out a vertebrate body part. The spinner also says "Hand" or "Foot" and "Left" or "Right." For example, the caller might say: "Right Hand, Eggs."

7. Players then put their correct hand or foot on a type of vertebrate that has that body part.

8. The first person to fall over or to put his or her hand or foot on the wrong type of vertebrate is the caller for the next round.

Parents' Tip

- Use the Players' Guide 1 (page 16) from the BONES bingo game to help players identify correct vertebrate characteristics.

ACTIVITY 3

Activity Journal

Of all the vertebrate groups, mammals have the most characteristics that are unique. *Unique* means that something is the only one of its kind. What vertebrate characteristics are unique to mammals?

_____

_____

_____

Do other types of vertebrates have unique characteristics? If so, what are they?

Amphibians _____

_____

_____

Birds _____

_____

_____

Fish _____

_____

_____

Reptiles _____

_____

_____

ACTIVITY 4

Critter Charades!

INSTRUCTIONS

Act out a vertebrate! What will you be today—a fish, amphibian, bird, reptile, or mammal?

MATERIALS

- Scissors
- Timer (up to 2 minutes)
- One or more friends or family members

1. Find at least one friend or family member to play with.

2. Cut out the Charades cards on page 47. Leave the second set of charades cards (page 49) uncut and use them as a guide to help players guess what is being acted.

3. Shuffle the cards and lay them face down.

4. Start the timer for two minutes and take turns drawing a card.

5. Without showing anyone your card, begin to act out your animal. Act out your animal without making any sounds!

6. Start by giving the guessers a clue as to what type of vertebrate you will act out:

If it's a(n):	Then do this action:
Amphibian	Leap like a frog.
Bird	Flap your arms like wings.
Fish	Make a fish face.
Mammal	Scratch under your armpits like a monkey.
Reptile	Stick out your tongue like a snake.

7. Guessers can ask yes or no questions. The actor can answer by nodding or shaking his or her head.

8. Whoever guesses the correct animal gets a point. If no one guesses, the actor loses a point. The person with the most points wins!

Parents' Tips

- It may be hard for kids to not make any noises. Consider bending the rules to suit your children.

- Aside from sideways Freddie the Flounder, don't all fish look the same? Consider a preliminary conversation about different fish and how to tell them apart. Do they live in lakes, rivers, or the ocean? Do you have any at home? Do they have different colors? Etc.

22

ACTIVITY 4

Experimental Journal

What was your favorite animal to act out? Why?

_____

_____

What type of vertebrate was hardest to act out? Why?

_____

_____

If you could be any type of vertebrate, what type would you be? Describe what your life would be like.

_____

_____

Curiosity Connector

Here are some links to help you follow your curiosity!

- If you thought these activities were interesting, you'll love to see these animals on video! The Web of Life has short videos of vertebrates AND invertebrates doing some of the most amazing things! Great for a rainy afternoon.
  http://shapeoflife.org/phyla

- Still a little confused about reptiles and amphibians? Can't remember if insects are vertebrates? Try your hand at these games for some clarification!
  http://www.pbslearningmedia.org/asset/lsps07_int_animalclass/

- Think you know what it takes to be a mammal, reptile, fish, bird, or amphibian? Try your hand at sorting the characteristics you've learned—and a few you haven't!
  http://www.sheppardsoftware.com/content/animals/kidscorner/games/animalclassgame.htm

- BrainPOP has some incredible cartoons and activities to test your animal knowledge. You have to pay for a lot of BrainPOP, but not this one!
  http://www.brainpopjr.com/science/animals/classifyinganimals/

- But where do the backbones come from? There's more to vertebrates than just their backbones. Watch this cartoon video to unlock the secret. And play a fun quiz!
  http://highered.mcgraw-hill.com/sites/dl/free/0078617022/167348/00038302.swf

- Vertebrate or invertebrate? Try sorting these animals with *National Geographic*.
  http://education.nationalgeographic.com/education/photo/vertebrate-invertebrate/?ar_a=1

- There are exceptions to every rule—even in science! See some of the world's strangest-looking animals and see if you can decide what kind of vertebrate they are—if they're even vertebrates at all!
  http://divaboo.info/

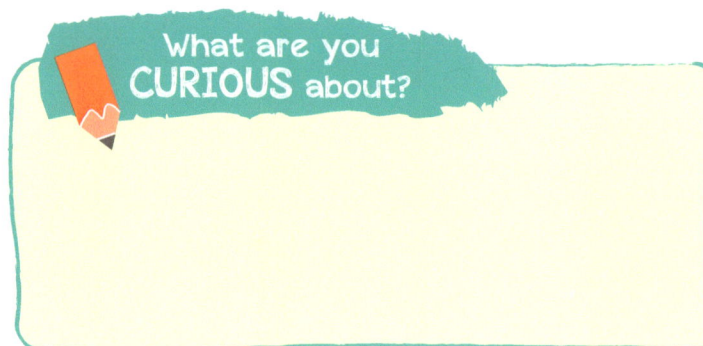

What are you CURIOUS about?

Glossary

AMPHIBIANS – Vertebrates that breathe with gills when they are young but grow lungs and lose their gills as adults. They are cold-blooded and lay eggs. Examples include frogs and toads.

BIRDS – Vertebrates that have feathers and lay eggs. They are warm-blooded. Examples include pigeons and penguins.

CHARACTERISTIC – Something that helps scientists identify an animal, such as scales or feathers.

FISH – Vertebrates that have scales and use gills to breathe. They are cold-blooded and usually lay eggs. Examples include salmon and anchovies.

INVERTEBRATES – Animals that don't have a backbone. Examples include jellyfish and insects.

MAMMALS – Vertebrates that use lungs to breathe, are warm-blooded, feed milk to their young from mammary glands, and have hair. Examples include people and whales.

REPTILES – Vertebrates that use lungs to breathe, are cold-blooded, and lay eggs. Examples include geckos and snakes.

VERTEBRATES – Animals that have a backbone.

Page 6 answers:
Vertebrates: camel, dolphin, fish, lizard, human, tiger, penguin, salamander, frog
Invertebrates: spider, butterfly, starfish, coral, slug

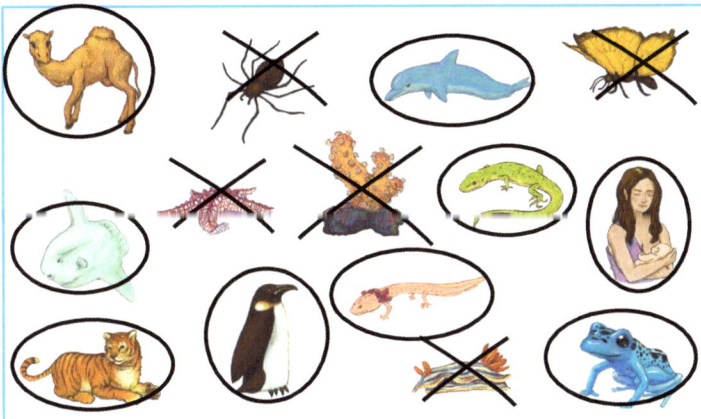

Tools for Your Tool Kit

Let's make the ideas you learned today part of your life tool kit. Remember to print out some blank tool kit pages and tape or glue on today's tools.

1. A vertebrate is an animal that has a _____ .

   Add a **BACKBONE** to your tool kit!

2. Which group of vertebrates has dry, scaly skin and is cold-blooded? _____

   Add a **REPTILE** to your tool kit!

3. Which group of vertebrates has feathers and lays eggs? _____

   Add a **BIRD** to your tool kit!

4. What type of vertebrate are you? Can you name another animal in this group?

   _____

   Add a **MAMMAL** to your tool kit!

5. Amphibians are special because they use _____ to breathe when

   they are young, and _____ to breathe air when they are older!

   Add an **AMPHIBIAN** to your tool kit!

6. Which group of vertebrates has scales and gills? _____

   Add a **FISH** to your tool kit!

Tools for Your Tool Kit (continued)

Backbone

Amphibian

Mammal

Reptile

Fish

Bird

cold-blooded

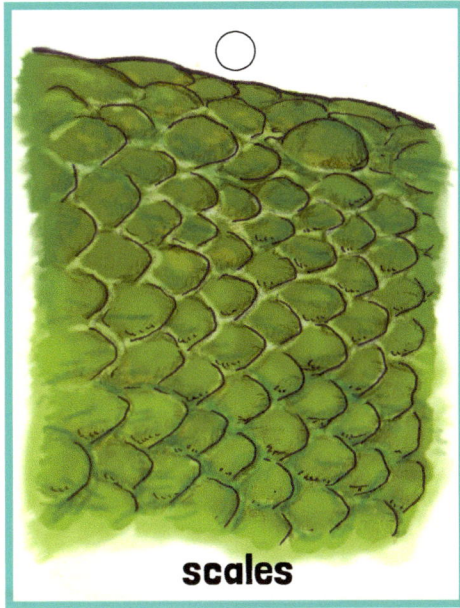

scales

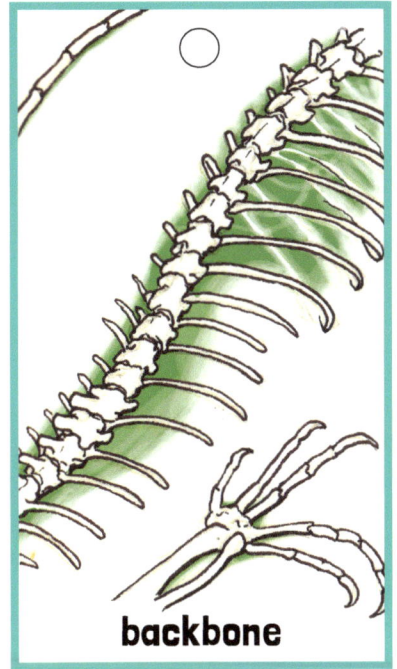

backbone

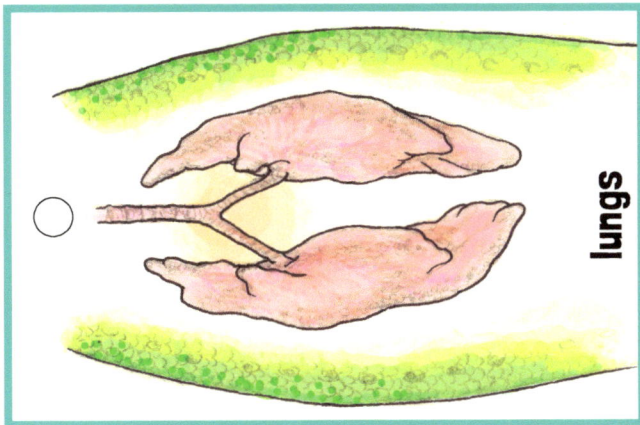

lungs

Reptiles

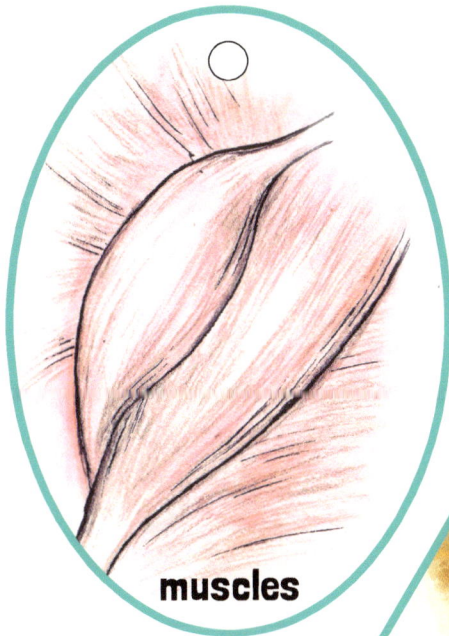

muscles

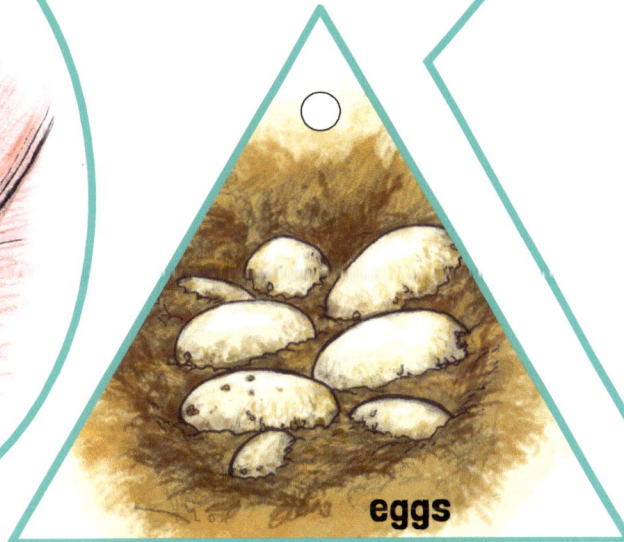

eggs

My favorite reptile:

_____

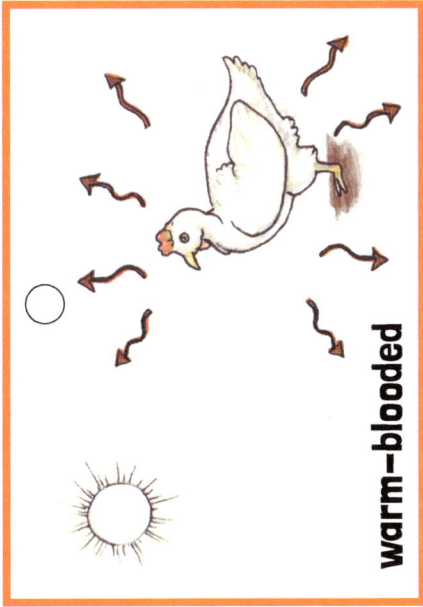

warm-blooded

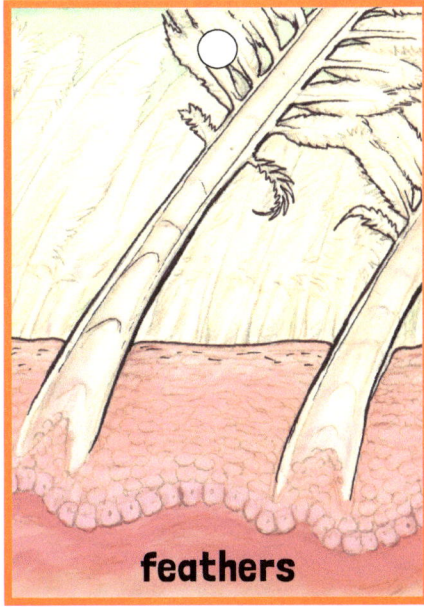

feathers

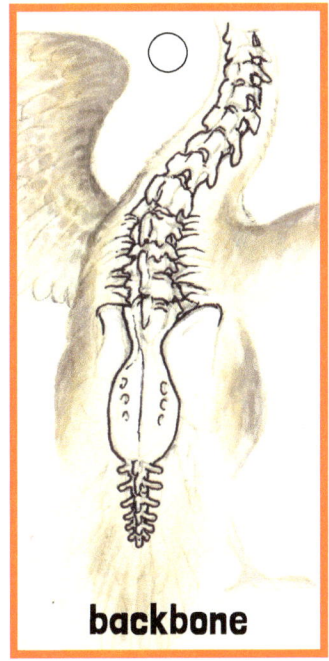

backbone

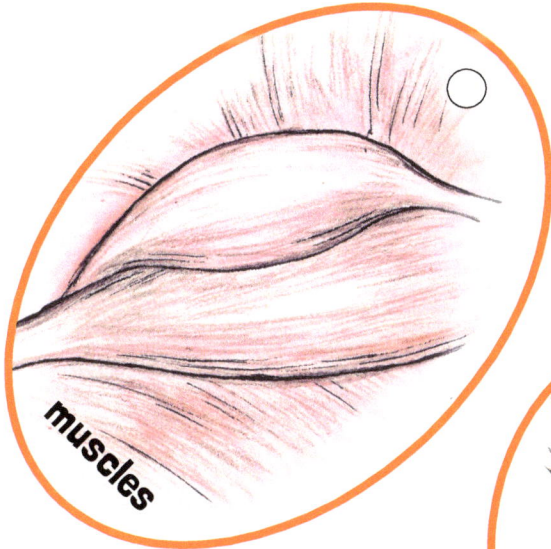

muscles

Birds

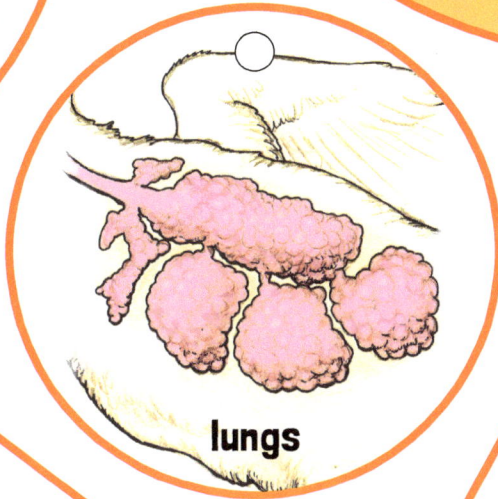

lungs

My favorite bird:

_____

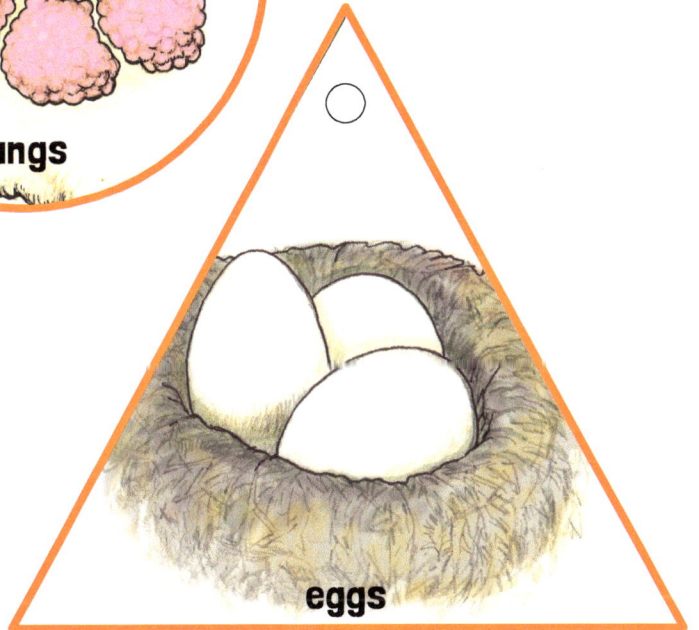

eggs

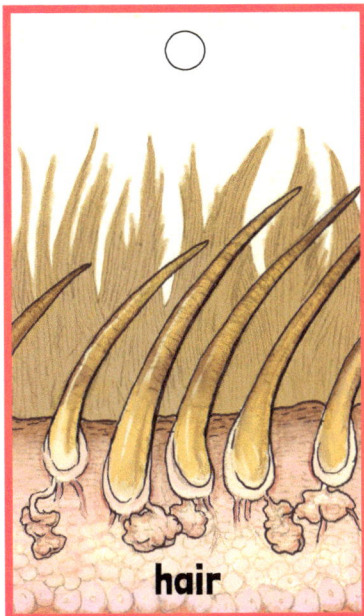

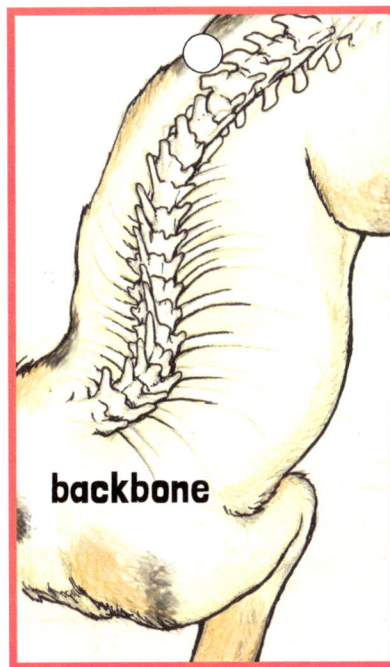

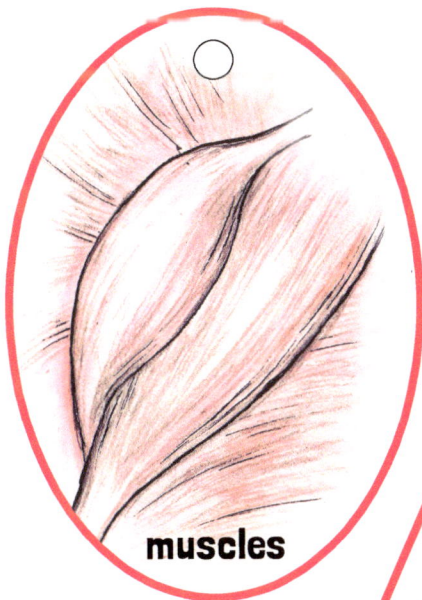

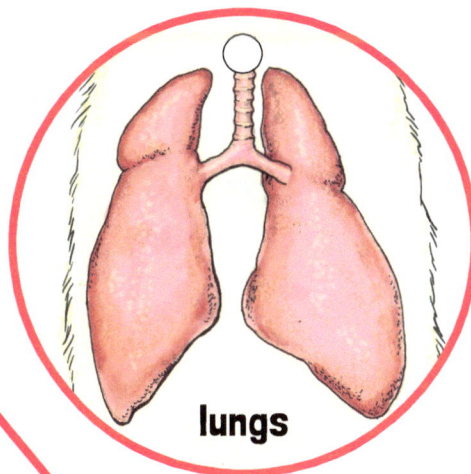

milk from mammary glands

hair

backbone

muscles

live young

lungs

Mammals

My favorite mammal:

_____

warm-blooded

33

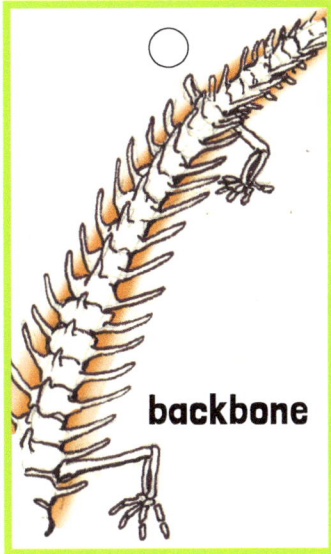

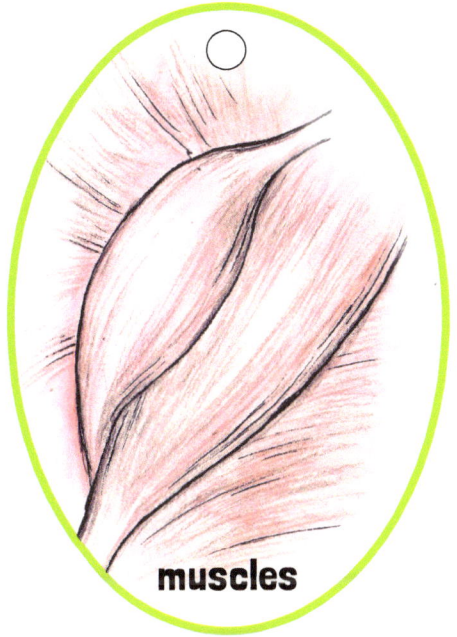

cold-blooded

backbone

muscles

Amphibians

gills

lungs

My favorite amphibian:

_____

eggs

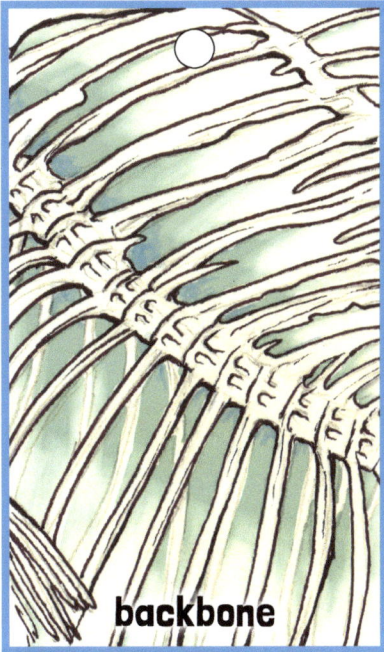

backbone

Fish

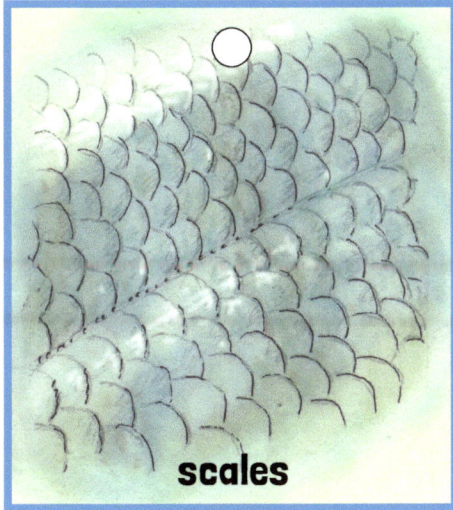

scales

cold-blooded

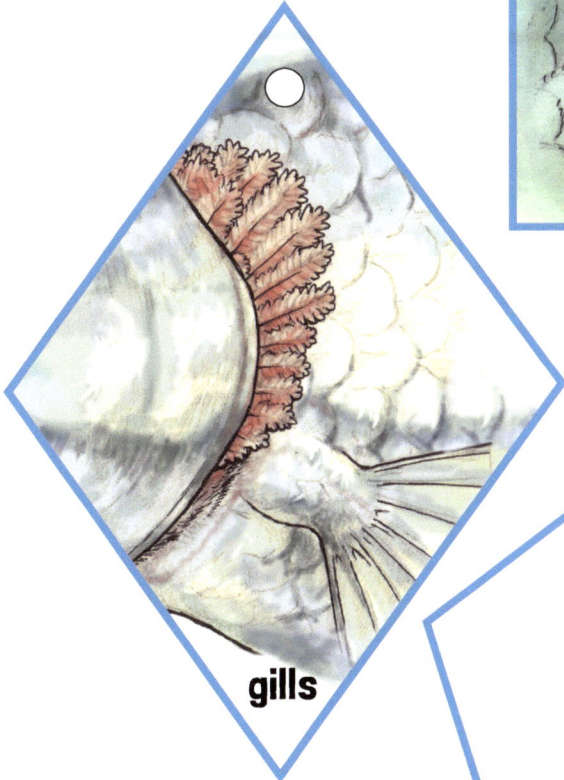

gills

My favorite fish:

_____

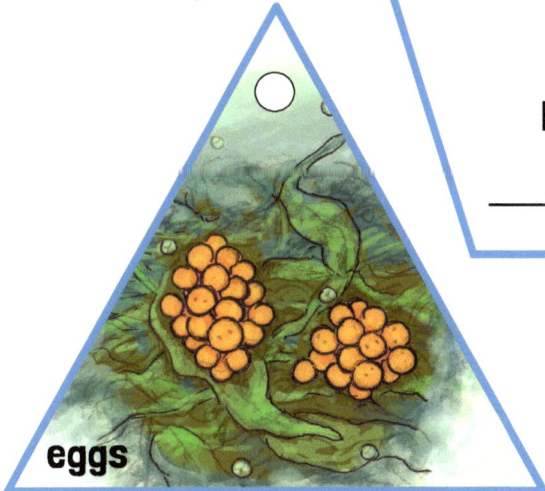

eggs

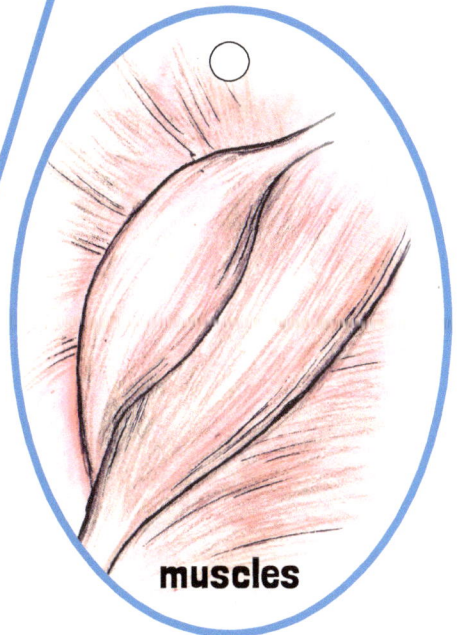

muscles

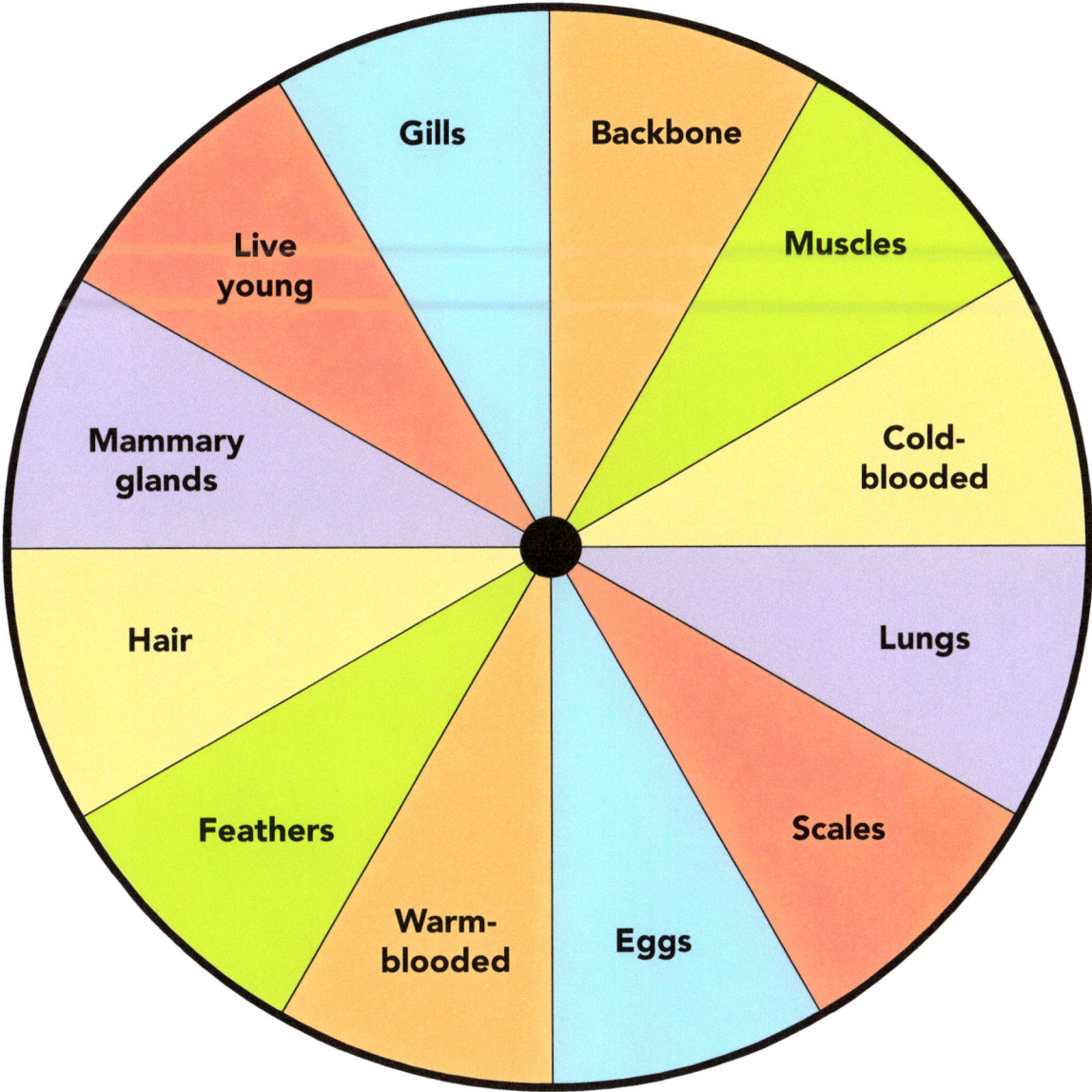

Game Card Cutouts for Activity 2: BONES Bingo

Card 1

B	O	N	E	S
Peeper Frog	Gecko	Blue Jay	Monkey	Whale
Mola Mola	Flamingo	Lizard	Puffer Fish	Rabbit
Legless Lizard	Dog	FREE!	Goldfish	Toad
Clownfish	Human	King Snake	Kangaroo	Flounder
Dolphin	Emu	Penguin	Newt	Brook Salamander

Card 2

B	O	N	E	S
Anaconda	Platypus	Owl	Poison Dart Frog	Angel Fish
Eel	Mudskipper	Crested Newt	Woodpecker	Komodo Dragon
Sea Turtle	Spotted Salamander	FREE!	Pelican	Hatchetfish
Sparrow	Cockatiel	American Crocodile	Shark	Softshell Turtle
Bullfrog	Bald Eagle	Pony	Thorny Devil	Tiger

Game Card Cutouts for Activity 2: BONES Bingo

B O N E S

B	O	N	E	S
Brook Salamander	Gecko	Crested Newt	Monkey	Whale
Mudskipper	Flamingo	Lizard	Kangaroo	Rabbit
Puffer Fish	Peeper Frog	FREE!	Komodo Dragon	Softshell Turtle
Blue Jay	Clownfish	King Snake	Dog	Legless Lizard
Dolphin	Emu	Penguin	Flounder	Human

B O N E S

B	O	N	E	S
Hatchetfish	Platypus	Shark	Poison Dart Frog	American Crocodile
Bullfrog	Tiger	Crested Newt	Woodpecker	Goldfish
Sea Turtle	Spotted Salamander	FREE!	Pelican	Eel
Sparrow	Cockatiel	Mola Mola	Anaconda	Toad
Angelfish	Bald Eagle	Pony	Thorny Devil	Owl

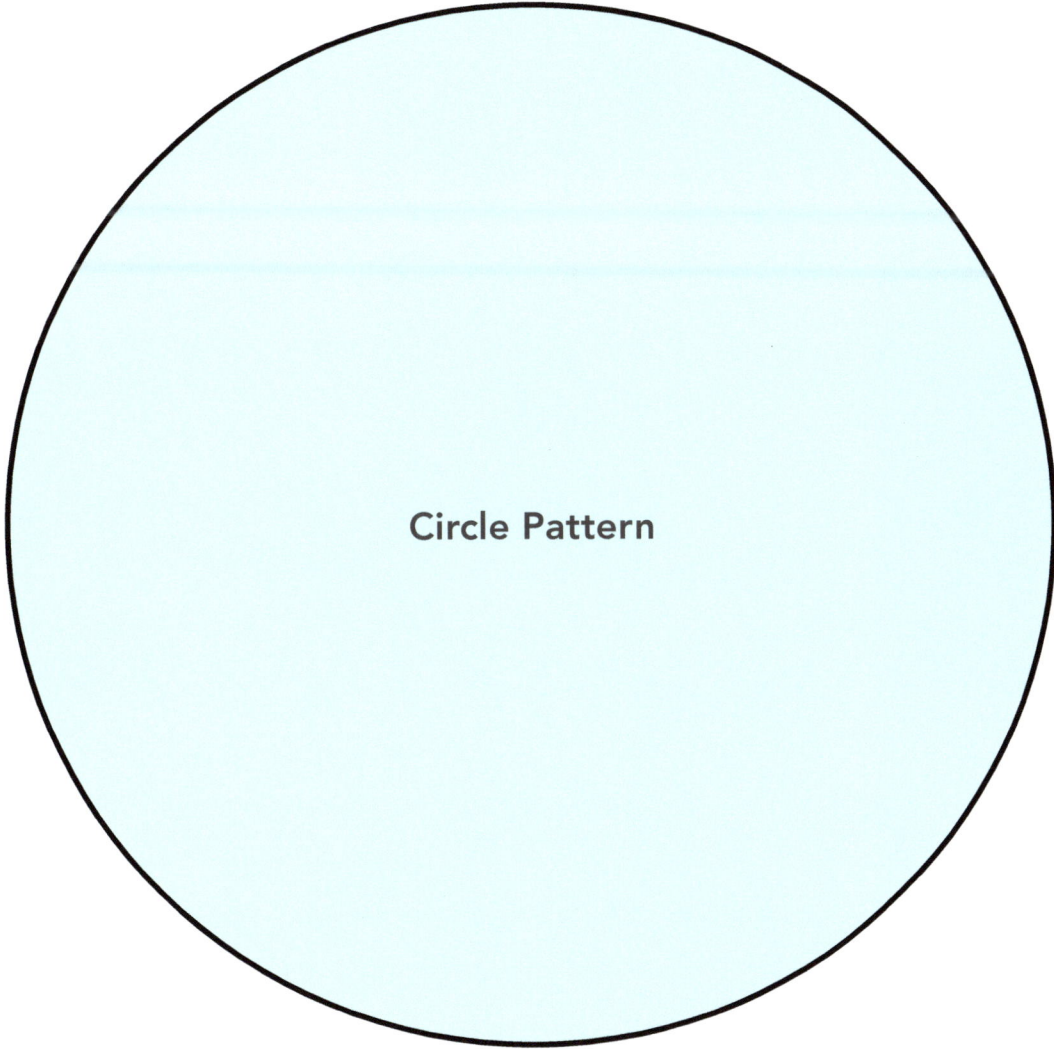

Circle Pattern

Owl • Is active at night • Eats mice and other small animals	**Ostrich** • Can't fly • The tallest and heaviest bird	**Penguin** • Can't fly but can swim • Eats fish	**Flamingo** • Lives in warm places • Is pink • Eats shrimp
Frog • Babies are tadpoles • Smooth skin • Eats flies	**Toad** • Babies are tadpoles • Bumpy skin • Lives in drier places	**Chameleon** • Changes color • Rotates its eyes	**Snake** • No legs • Can eat small (and sometimes large!) animals whole • Lives in trees or on or under the ground
Dog • Walks on all fours • Wags its tail • A popular pet	**Dolphin** • Lives in the ocean • Eats fish • Is very smart	**Kangaroo** • Baby lives in mother's pouch • Hops instead of walking	**Monkey** • Lives in trees or on the ground • Grooms its friends • Carries its babies on its back
Flounder • Flat fish • Swims on its side • Two eyes on the same side of its head	**Clownfish** • Lives in an anemone • Orange and white stripes • Lives in warm waters	**Barracuda** • Long, skinny fish • Big teeth • Bright silver color • Lives in warm water	**Mudskipper** • Can breathe out of water for a short time • Lives in muddy places • Uses front fins to walk
Create Your Own!	**Create Your Own!**	**Create Your Own!**	**Create Your Own!**

Owl • Is active at night • Eats mice and other small animals	**Ostrich** • Can't fly • The tallest and heaviest bird	**Penguin** • Can't fly but can swim • Eats fish	**Flamingo** • Lives in warm places • Is pink • Eats shrimp
Frog • Babies are tadpoles • Smooth skin • Eats flies	**Toad** • Babies are tadpoles • Bumpy skin • Lives in drier places	**Chameleon** • Changes color • Rotates its eyes	**Snake** • No legs • Can eat small (and sometimes large!) animals whole • Lives in trees or on or under the ground
Dog • Walks on all fours • Wags its tail • A popular pet	**Dolphin** • Lives in the ocean • Eats fish • Is very smart	**Kangaroo** • Baby lives in mother's pouch • Hops instead of walking	**Monkey** • Lives in trees or on the ground • Grooms its friends • Carries its babies on its back
Flounder • Flat fish • Swims on its side • Two eyes on the same side of its head	**Clownfish** • Lives in an anemone • Orange and white stripes • Lives in warm waters	**Barracuda** • Long, skinny fish • Big teeth • Bright silver color • Lives in warm water	**Mudskipper** • Can breathe out of water for a short time • Lives in muddy places • Uses front fins to walk
Create Your Own!	**Create Your Own!**	**Create Your Own!**	**Create Your Own!**

science Tool Kit